PRESS ON IN HOPE

• THE LORD IS MY SHEPHERD •

CAROL N GOODE

Ark House Press
arkhousepress.com

© 2022 Carol N Goode

All rights reserved. Apart from any fair dealing for the purpose of study, research, criticism, or review, as permitted under the Copyright Act, no part may be reproduced by any process without written permission.

Unless otherwise stated, all Scriptures are taken from the New International Translation (Holy Bible. Copyright© 1996, 2004, 2007, 2013 by Tyndale House Foundation. Used by permission of Tyndale House Publishers Inc., Carol Stream, Illinois 60188. All rights reserved.)

Some names and identifying details have been changed to protect the privacy of individuals.

Cataloguing in Publication Data:
Title: Press On In Hope
ISBN: 978-0-6455397-2-1 (pbk)
Subjects: Christian Living; Faith;
Other Authors/Contributors: Goode, Carol N;

Cover image courtesy of bengoode.com.au taken at Mount Lofty S.A.
Design by initiateagency.com

Acknowledgement

For all those who challenged, inspired and encouraged me along a difficult path. The many twists and turns often seemed to hold no purpose-except to hang on in faith to the One who has already planned the journey.

Thanks

"Thanks be to God for His indescribable gift."
(1Corinthians 9:15)

Chosen To Win

When darkness and derision surround

me like a fog.

When the goal post fades from

sight.

I *will* my heart to recall God's

truth.

Chosen to win!

Indeed the battle has already been

won.

Press on in hope!

Introduction

The title of this book is PRESS ON based on the example of the Prophet Enoch. A faithful Preacher of righteousness. The details of his life take up less space than my introduction.

'**...Enoch *walked* with God...and was no more...**' (Genesis 5:18-21)

A significant quote from the Book of Enoch by Enoch is recorded in the Book of Jude v.14. It refers to God's final judgement and the need of God's people to be vigilant and ready. Several other quotes in both the Old Testament and the New Testament are also recorded.

What does it mean to actually WALK with the Lord? More importantly, to walk *faithfully* with the Lord. To **walk in Spirit and in Truth**. This challenge was first put to myself. My prayer is that others will also be challenged by the same question. Perhaps even surprised by the answer.

Maybe you are curious about the things of God and simply want to know more. Most people I know desire more than empty religion without power. I know I do. When we are genuinely earnest in going deeper, God always shows up. He provides the insight and ecouragement to PRESS ON as we press into His presence and embrace His plans.

To walk faithfully before God in these troubling times is truly the hope that does not disappoint. My source is God's Word. My hope is in Christ Himself, the true light of the world who brings all things to completion.

The Alpha and the Omega. The beginning and the end.

Contents

Chapter 1. Walking In Hope   1

Chapter 2. Walking In Faith   5

Chapter 3. Keeping Pace   10

Chapter 4. Walking In Grace   16

Chapter 5. Walking In Love   20

Chapter 6. Walking In Encouragement   28

Chapter 7. Walking As One   31

Chapter 8. Watch And Pray   36

Chapter 9. The Whole Armour Of God   43

Chapter 10. Walking In Freedom   48

Chapter 11. Walking In Spirit And Truth   54

Chapter 12. Walking In Wisdom   62

Chapter 13. Rejoice Always   72

Chapter 14. Rest In The Lord   76

Chapter 15. The Lord Is My Shepherd   80

Chapter One

WALKING IN HOPE

'The Lord is my light and my salvation; whom shall I be afraid...'
Psalm 27:1

The idea for this book began to take shape February 2020. A year hard to forget. The year of our introduction to the Covid-19 virus to an unprepared world; claiming lives and smashing economies. The many challenges to the normal flow of a pleasure seeking world, continues even as I write.

One of the noticeable side effects of this Covid-19 pandemic for many is anxiety and a feeling of helplessness. The enforcement of lockdowns, has become a double-edged sword. Yes, to protect the vulnerable. However, the marked spike in suicides and mental health issues reveal balance and sensibility has not always prevailed. Despite the recent roll out of vaccination supplies, and their hopeful preventative abilities, Covid-19 still remains the invisible enemy bent on changing our lives forever...

On the plus side. Many are learning new and creative ways to operate in both business and church areas. Families have reconnected by doing creative things together while in confinement. The benefit of putting the needs of others in place of our own keeps us all moving in the same direction.

Technology is certainly helping advance the Gospel and reaching the many unchurched. The boundaries of old institutional molds are being extended. Terms like zoom and church-at-home keep us attached when face to face meetings are not advisable. After all, God's church was never meant to be just a comfortable nest for helpless fledglings sitting in pews. The challenge to learn to fly and depend on Christ Himself is surely a positive thing.

There are certainly varying opinions regarding the origin (and purpose) of this pandemic. The real truth still remains carefully concealed. A swirl of conspiracy theories keep arising from this lack of information. Well may we all be in this together but where exactly are we being taken? Persistent coercion from those in power whom we are meant to trust, calls for WISDOM.

It is also a time when free speech has become increasingly under threat. Critical thinking, fair debate and certainly religious freedoms are increasingly being challenged. A Christian can now be quickly maligned for simply daring to speak God's truth. It seems righteousness itself is fast becoming a Capital Offense. This is not a time for Christians to be caught napping.

I am certainly thankful that God's Word is more up to date than today's newspaper or global newsbyte! In the midst of all these challenges.

Jesus Christ is the same yesterday, today and forever...' (Hebrews 13:8)

Amidst this concentration on Covid related challenges it is becoming increasingly apparent how short we are on good role models. Today, Television and Sporting celebrities plus more than a few Politicians, seem bent on a race to the bottom. An indulgent generation wearing arrogance and pride as their badge to fame.

To walk with dignity and steadfastness in the light of one's calling, whether it be for Queen or the King of Kings is surely commendable on any level.

Enoch the Prophet of God born 328 BC had a short but powerful testimony recorded in Genesis 5:21

*Enoch **walked** with God: and he was no more; for God took him.*

Enoch is recorded as living for 365 years. It is clear through other references that although confronted with rampart ungodliness he did not shrink from proclaiming truth.

The Hebrew meaning of the word WALK ('Halak') is to live following a manner of life. Enoch pleased God because his heart was fixed on living a righteous life in an unrighteous world. His bent was towards the things of God despite many around being bound by earthly concerns. He refused to allow himself to be molded by the world and its inclinations.

His heart was set on remaining faithful to a faithful God who keeps His promises.

A true Prophet's lot is not an easy one in any generation. The role of the Prophet is to confront people with truth regardless of popular outcome. Enoch was not a soothsayer or an appeaser bending to the favour of those around him. The false Prophets of his day (as with our day) often sought to flatter with oracles of false hope. They were rarely rejected because they told the hearer what they wanted to hear. Sound familiar?

How thankful I am that Christ is my Saviour and Lord. My great High Priest and Wonderful Counsellor. The King of Kings and Lord of Lords! My rock and fortress. My strength and protection in the shadow of His wings. The Good Shepherd of truth who leads me beside the still waters of His love and grace.

This powerful rallying call of hope remains secure amidst all the changes and trials of life. God has a plan and purpose not just for us individually but for the world in general. Nothing is outside of His control. Nothing catches Him by surprise. The sovereign Lord of the Universe still reigns and His purpose is secure. Just keep walking…

*'And now what do I wait for? **My hope is in you alone.**'* (Psalm 39:7)

PRESS ON in hope

CHAPTER TWO

WALKING IN FAITH

'Now faith is the substance of things hoped for: the evidence of things not seen.' (Hebrew 11:1)

The Epistle to the Hebrews was written in AD mid-60s. The epistle was written to challenge a group of fragile believers to persevere in their commitment to Christ rather than drift away into unbelief. The FAITH theme is unmistakable and speaks to all Christians down through the ages.

A good reason alone to make it a focus in this chapter. The reader is urged to familiarize and meditate again on this power packed letter in the Book of Hebrews.

Saving faith is granted through faith on the finished work of Christ on the cross; His death and resurrection. It is not our own doing but the gift of God. Certainly not faith in ourselves or even in the power of prayer or our own words.

It is Faith in Christ Himself to do everything according to His great mercy and purposes, exceeding all that we can ask, think or even imagine.

God in His great sovereignty follows His own script. He removes and allows according to His own wonderous purposes. He only asks that we walk closely beside Him, allowing His plans and our understanding merge as one. There will be times when understanding fails us. Perhaps it is then that we truly activate faith as outlined in the Book of Hebrews.

The great Patriarch Abraham did not question God when faced with preparing his own promised son as a sacrifice. He chose to obey and found God to be both merciful and trustworthy in His promises. FAITH.

It is also true that in matters of faith, many Christians feel safe and happy with saving faith but remain cautious and sometimes unbelieving when it comes to genuine miraculous activity. However, when God's Word states that *'Jesus Christ is the same today, yesterday and forever.'* I believe It means exactly that.

Our theological pendulum has the tendency to swing from one religious extreme to another.

However, I was greatly encouraged to read a testimony in CHALLENGE, the Good News Paper No. 446 which I believe revealed a good balance. The pendulum landed in the middle.

(The following account is a condensed version)

It began in 2004 with nosebleeds. When it progressed to blinding headaches and fainting spells, Jason Ong knew something was very wrong.

Doctors informed him that he had a rare form of brain cancer with only about 200 cases worldwide. At 31 and into only three years of his marriage it was a crushing blow. He was told he had only 6 months to live. His condition steadily deteriorated.

Jason had experienced first hand many miracles in his life. His own conversion while at the death bed of his father and also his marriage to Judith, hold a wonderful testimony of God's grace and healing in themselves. However, the pain and regression of this prognosis had become so unbearable, death seemed his only release.

He did consent to another operation but when he awoke he could barely see and breathing was unbearably painful. He finally asked his wife to let him die.

"I am so tired. I just want to go home."

His wife Judith would not give up but prayed fervently. This same midnight Judith woke up to the sound of her husband crying out. "Jesus is here! Jesus is here" and trembling so hard his bed shook. Feeling a hand touch him, he heard Jesus say to him.

"I am moved by the tears of your wife. I will heal you." Jason breathed in a deep breath, whispered, "Thank you Jesus", and fell asleep.

When he woke up the next morning, he found he could see, breath and walk. There was no pain. Against all odds he was discharged the next day.

There is still a little of the tumor left in Jason's brain but the debilitating symptoms are now gone.

"Praise the Lord. He has healed me," the Hong Kong Restauranteur says with a smile. Both he and his wife continue with their work and also bless others with their feeding programs for the underprivileged. I believe Jason's own statement sums up very adequately the meaning of FAITH.

Scripture says, "to live is Christ, to die is gain. I know my life is not my own and I have chosen to live this life to be a blessing to others."

His experience with cancer has given Jason a sober message. "When I minister to the sick, I tell them.

'If Jesus heals you, hallelujah. If He dosen't you must be ready to meet Him.'

The pendulum sits in the middle.

God is certainly able to heal and deliver us today from sin and sickness. Is anything too hard for the living God of the Universe? And yet He alone decides what is best according to His own purposes. The sovereign God of the Universe!

Another thought struck me rather forcibly as I read Jason's testimony.

We must never give up on those we are entrusted to pray for. Some may reach a point where they are unable to have the strength to go on. To be with the Lord infinitely more preferable. We do not always know the mind of Christ in every situation but our faith through prayer on behalf of another is always heard.

Not all situations in our walk of faith present so dramatically as the above account. Nor do they always end with the same desired outcome. Here too, the purposes of God should be received in faith.

Another equally important truth is that faith muscles are largely developed through trials and adversity. Walking through long seasons of drought and uncertainty also demands faith which in return produces endurance. Thus the title of this book. **PRESS ON!**

It takes bold faith to give thanks in *every* situation!

A powerful illustration of faith was provided beautifully by Jesus Christ Himself. The disciples had started to obsess about who was the greatest in the Kingdom O God. I'm sure His answer raised more than a few eyebrows.

'Assuredly, I say to you, unless you are converted and become as little children, you will by no means enter the Kingdom of Heaven. Therefore whoever humbles himself as this little child is the greatest in the Kingdom of Heaven.' (Matthew 18:2-4)

He uses the innocence of small children as an example of the type of faith He is looking for.

"Little children naturally exercise a beautiful faith. Until the adults around them introduce fear into their lives, they have no difficulty in believing what they cannot see. " (Verity Kew)

To walk in faith means to trust implicitly the One whom we are called to follow. Let us not lose heart. Let us not lose focus. Jesus Christ Himself is the pioneer and perfecter of our faith.

PRESS ON in faith and do not lose heart.

Chapter Three

KEEPING PACE

"The race is not to the swift, nor the battle to the strong..." (Ecclesiastes 9:11)

This is good news for those of us who do not fall under either of the above categories.

Keeping pace in an uncertain world that can quickly change, demands spiritual stamina. There is no right pace because we are all different and formed for unique circumstances. However, walking in calmness and confidence prepares us for the inevitable twists and turns.

While meditating on the many verses in the Bible that reference the word WALK, the following verse popped into my mind and then refused to leave. I hadn't heard or even thought about it for some time so it seemed significant.

"See then that you walk circumspectly, not as fools but as wise, redeeming the time, because the days are evil..." (Ephesians 5:15)

I scrambled for my Bible to find the context. What does the word *circumspect* actually mean? I must have quoted it several times at some point in my Christian walk but the word had rolled off my tongue without any great depth of thought. That's the thing about diamonds we can thoughtlessly walk over them many times but only when we get out our shovels and do some serious digging do we discover their intrinsic beauty and value.

The best commentary I could find came from: **timeintheword.com**

"To walk circumspectly is to walk with great care, accuracy and precision. This involves taking deliberate and carefully thought out steps. It is not running or rushing. It is not walking in a manner where we do not know where we are going."

The rest of this verse is also worth examining.

wisdom is knowing the right thing to do in each given situation.

Redeeming the time refers to not allowing ourselves to become distracted or side tracked. How encouraging to know that despite some powerfully tempting diversions out there, there is also hope and forgiveness when we do sin or get side tracked.

Wow!

It suddenly made sense to me why the past week I had suffered some sort of mysterious swelling in my right ankle that had forced me to limp and favour my left ankle. It slowed me down considerably and forced me to rely heavily upon what I like to call my Moses stick. Originally used as a snake alert on long walks with my dog Corrie but now my leaning frame to allow my right ankle to heal.

In the past I had always operated on two buttons - fast or stop. I seem to have chosen a dog with a similar temperament. A brisk walk around the block is never going to suffice. The alternative is lots of open space, hilly terrain plus rocky and uneven paths.

I remember as a child the constant reminder that I was " rough on shoes." I had a tendency to walk hard on my heels with a slight tilt to one side. I never quite grew out of this and suspect this swelling which has now gone down, is that same tendency to walk hard in rough places without much thought or care.

I do not think it stretching to say. This foot pain on the physical level is similar to the above verse on a spiritual level.

The challenge to walk wisely and redeem the time poses another equally important question and follows hard on the heels of the above verse. How do we find and know God's personal will in our life?

Do we sit quietly with folded hands and eyes upwards toward Heaven? Sometimes.

Do we wait for a sheet to come down from Heaven with clear instructions before moving? Rarely.

Do we hop into a boat and push it out to sea (figuratively speaking!) hoping we will be directed or redirected so long as we keep moving? Sometimes.

My point here is that many of us want a fool-proof formulae but there is none. This is why religion is so popular and *walking in Spirit and truth* the less travelled road. Finding God's personal will in our lives actually means finding God's pace and sticking with Him.

Walking circumspectly.

The establishment of a regular habit of meditating on the Scriptures and personal prayer for daily guidance demands discipline. It is easy to get side tracked or rely largely on the opinions of others rather than the Word of God.

In times when stress and sometimes my own impetuousness take hold, I am reminded afresh.

"*...**In quietness and confidence shall be your strength...**"* (Isaiah 30:14)

No doubt He knows me intimately enough to know that quietness and confidence are not my natural strengths. How comforting to also know that He is the One who gives grace, preparation and completion.

"For by grace you have been saved through faith, and that not of yourselves: it is the gift of God, not of works lest anyone should boast. For we are His workmanship created in Christ Jesus for good works, which God prepared beforehand that we should walk in them." (Ephesians 2: 8-10)

It is the Holy Spirit who guides us into all truth according to God's written Word. How easy to overlook or totally ignore another equally important role. To fill us with power and equip us with everything we need to fulfill His purpose not our own. Our heavenly Father waits to be invited into the centre of our lives. This is always His will regardless of place or station.

Alongside this truth, we are all called to be His witnesses. We have the power to elevate His name or debase it. The following thought took hold of me powerfully while recently driving to church.

There is no doubt the world outside of Christ lies under God's judgement. His church also sits on trial: especially as the Day of His Appearing draws closer. However, there are some sitting and watching this trial with more than a little interest. They are secretly hoping - actually willing us to win. They want to believe that what we say, and who we are, can also set them free!

This truth shook my being so powerfully I almost went through a red light. Not such a good ending for such a powerful truth! It did remind me afresh of the point.

We may be the only Bible some people will ever read. Let's determine to give them a *good* read.

Not all are called into specialized ministries that involve preaching and evangelism. However, every Christian is called to bear witness to Him in our everyday lives.

I personally do not enjoy shopping so I have time to observe while my husband Jack completes the shopping on his motorized shopper. Everyone has a different shopping pace which shows clearly on their faces. Add to this, the extra diligence to hand sanitization, validating codes, following arrows, correct spacing and endless recordings reminding us of all these obligations. Any sense of individualism or intimacy is now a luxury.

My point? Our goal reveals our priorities and the pace we determine shows. It shows on our faces and is reflected in our response to those around us.

Who we really are when we THINK NOBODY IS WATCHING.

Sometimes I even catch myself out. That muffled sigh of exasperation. The brief scowl of annoyance. The lost chance of curbing my impatience and ignoring small curtisies.

It is also not uncommon to have a complete personality change when placed behind a steering wheel! Yes indeed we all have our 'tipping points.'

However, it is here in the cut and thrust of these circumstances that God can teach us our finest lessons. *Patience, compassion, longsuffering and humility*. Fruits of the Holy Spirit.

When we allow the world's mold to determine our pace it is easy to forget God's grace. Definitely much easier to be diverted from the main path and miss out on God's best.

I enjoy walking amongst nature and sometimes minor trails can be a great source of temptation. Sometimes I enjoy them, simply because I think they may prove to be a shortcut. Mostly they're not! Sometimes the very path itself can be a painful reminder. It may indeed be a shortcut but the painful trail of thorns leading to it is going to be more memorable than the shortcut itself.

Other times the very expectation of finding something new and exciting becomes a tempting diversion.

I learnt the other day that there is actually a name for these minor paths. '**Desire paths'**. They take you where your heart desires, rather than where the main path tries to direct you.

Mmnn.

PRESS ON…Keeping pace with our Maker does require discipline. It also provides protection and security.

Chapter Four

WALKING IN GRACE

"For God so loved the world that He gave His only begotten Son, that whoever believes in Him should not perish but have everlasting life..." (John 3:16...)

We cannot comprehend properly the extent of God's grace unless we understand what we have been saved from. God is a Holy and Just God who cannot look on sin and the only way to deal with it once and for all is through the freewill sacrifice of His only begotten Son. The sinless sacrifice made available to all who receive Christ and call upon Him in faith.

The only door into His presence to receive salvation is personal faith in the finished work of the cross. Through His death, resurrection and ascension we are delivered from everlasting torment and granted through faith eternal life.

Hell was originally designed for satan and his fallen Angels but when disobedience came into the world through Adam, freewill came into play. Man could receive by faith God's offer of salvation or refuse it. No one is sent to hell. People choose hell because they choose to reject God's offer of salvation.

We are not robots. Genuine love means having a choice. His grace and love is offered to everyone. He is not willing that any should perish but all should come to repentance.

We seem to have become increasing light on the 'h' word. The word 'hell' is offensive to many including some believers and even some Theologians. Why?

Part of the reason is that it is easy to fall into the trap of trying to make God into our own image rather than embrace the inconvenient truth. We are made in God's image.

The same tactic employed by satan in the Garden of Eden is still in vogue today. Namely to seduce us into thinking that God is holding out on us. Why shouldn't we become our own little god and control our own destiny. This is the very seductive thinking that New Age teaching has employed for many years. It feeds into our PRIDE; the lie that we can make God into our own image and then think we can get away with it.

God is a Holy God and our ticket to holiness can only be through His Son Jesus Christ.

Perhaps this is the first time you have fully understood the connection between a Holy God and His marvelous grace in sending His Son Jesus Christ to be our sin bearer?

People often look confused when I make the statement.

"I'm a Christian but I'm not religious." It has proven to be a good conversation opener for those genuinely searching.

Religion is reaching up to God and trying to attain His standard. A Christian is someone who recognizes their inability to reach a Holy God through their own effort. Jesus Christ is the One who reaches down. Thanks be to Christ Jesus, His salvation is available to all who receive Him through faith.

"For by grace we are saved through faith and this not of yourselves; it is the gift of God, not of works lest anyone should boast." (Ephesians 2:8)

New teachings and philosophies are constantly attempting to rearrange God's express narrative written in His Word. Why? To draw us off from the main track leading us into compromise and lukewarm Christianity.

Thankfully, we are also promised the Holy Spirit. The presence of God within to guide, protect, comfort, interpret and discipline. Through the Holy Spirit we are able to plug into the very power resource of God Himself!

Now that should be Good News alone!

Some Christians reading this book may have started well but have now fallen back into trying to keep the letter of the law through rules and regulations. Legalism may feed our misplaced feelings of self righteousness but that's all! The letter destroys. It is the Spirit that gives grace and life.

Further, If you have never come to the place where you have the choice to forgive (show grace) then you have lived a truly remarkable life! Our journey with Christ is surely littered with opportunities to walk in grace and forgiveness. Despite our feelings sometimes demanding a different message, the command to FORGIVE remains.

We live and move under the grace of a God who has given all. Whenever we show forgiveness we reflect His image and receive His peace. Forgiveness is not an optional extra. It is the very core of our walk with the Lord. The Lord's Prayer in **Matthew 6: 10-13** and Christ's admonition in v14 reveal the vital connection between grace and forgiveness.

We cannot understand grace without understanding God's holiness. We cannot understand Heaven without also acknowledging hell. God came in human flesh through His Son Jesus Christ. The lamb of God who took away sin once for all-available to all- could enjoy His presence evermore.

I did not set out to present grace in the above terms but I strongly believe there is no point in pressing on in Christ while carrying the heavy weight of sin due to unbelief. An unnecessary burden designed to cause us to stumble before we reach the finishing line.

PRESS ON in the assurance of this foundational truth called GRACE.

Chapter Five

WALKING IN LOVE

"But if we walk in the light as He is in the light, we have fellowship with one another, and the blood of Jesus Christ His Son cleanses us from all sin." (1John 1: 7)

The original title of this chapter was 'Walking in Transparency' followed by the chapter title 'Walking in Light'. Instead I have decided to tie the three themes together under the one heading. LOVE. Three connected themes tied together releasing a pleasing aroma of GRACE.

The love that Christ highlights is AGAPE love. A love that surpasses earthly and even brotherly love. It is a love that seeks that highest good in every person. It is the sacrificial love Christ Himself provided through His death on a cross.

"But God demonstrates His own love towards us, that even when we were still sinners, Christ died for us." (Romans 5:8)

The quality of this love shines into our very being. It both sees our need and covers it with grace. It is both transparent and slow to judge. The challenge here, is for us mere humans to exhibit this same grace. This same love. This same transparency to all those He places within our path.

The word transparency according to the OXFORD dictionary:

that can be clearly seen through. allowing light to pass through without diffusion (of disguise, pretext etc.) Easily seen through, obvious, easily understood.

I suspect some will find TRANSPARENCY more challenging than pleasing. I do not apologize. Truth often hurts and whatever I have written know that many like myself have had to pass through the cleansing fire of transparency. Naked before the Lord and harder still - others. It is the 'others' that can bring us undone more quickly and sting us with their judgements. And just as easy we can sting others with our own judgements.

I cannot say I have personally always emerged from this particular challenge unscathed but I will pause here and provide several situations in my own life which showed me the importance of WALKING IN LOVE. The kind of love that is sincere and transparent.

The first one happened in a small group session aligned to a fellowship my Husband and I attended earlier in our marriage. This Holy Spirit revival was not planned nor expected-at least by ourselves.

We had merely come together to pray for our church and each other. What followed after the first 15 or so minutes of prayer took us all by surprise. Many started to confess their own sins followed by others confessing their hidden resentments towards each other. There were many genuine tears of repentance and renewed relationships that had floundered in secret were put right.

It was in essence a genuine revival. It came from an honesty and TRANSPARENCY Before God- linked to our need to be honest and transparent with each other. It was not created by human effort but a genuine work of the Holy Spirit who blessed our meeting with His own presence.

Most of the details including my own response are thankfully a little foggy. I suspect the main thing we were all meant to carry with us was not each others hidden secrets brought to the light. It was the powerful truth that when we are emptied of self He fills us with Himself!

Nothing of ourselves we bring. simply to the cross we cling!!

I would love to say that the result from this small revival permeated the whole church. In some parts it may have but on a different level. Sadly it was not long before the Leaders tried to harness this surprise visitation and replace it with well meaning goals and programmes. These did hold some value but the work begun in the Holy Spirit was soon quenched and put aside for something less.

I also have pleasant memories of my time spent as a volunteer Counsellor in a Telephone Counselling Ministry called LIVING HOPE. The experience of working with fellow counsellors from a cross section of church affiliations was both stretching and encouraging. Stretching because we all came from different Christian perpectives. Encouraging because somehow it still worked and good fruit was continually evident. Praying at the commencement and conclusion of each shift for each other and those we ministered to through the phone contacts kept everything flowing smoothly. Our role was to listen, offer counsel and present the Gospel when an opportunity presented itself. Only when we veered from this focus did problems arise.

I'm sure we didn't get everything right all the time. However, I do believe God blessed this unity in the Spirit and the genuine desire to serve Him faithfully.

Although Living Hope Inc was set up as an outreach to the unchurched and those searching, it also became a safe base for people who had experienced spiritual abuse within the church. I have to say, a very large proportion of my calls contained hurt and sometimes bitter Christians who no longer trusted church as a safe place. It was a chance for me to listen non judgmentally and offer the only hope I had at my disposable according to God's Word. Spiritual abuse was real. I knew this first hand. I also knew the only hope of dealing with it is through FORGIVENESS. This forgiveness had to come from the will as reconciliation in many cases appeared irrepairable. Only from this base could the wounded be set free to move on and embrace the next chapter in their lives. Forgiveness is not an optional extra. It is a Divine directive.

We cannot know true freedom in Christ if our hearts are weighed down with a bitterness or unforgiveness. The person we hurt the most is not only ourselves but more importantly our precious Saviour. He forgave while we too were sinners in need of His forgiveness and grace.

On the other side of grace I can recall a time in my church life when being in agreement (or at least showing respect) proved a bridge too far.

This particular Deaconess in the church had certainly earned her stripes through dedication, and extremely good organisational skills. A dominating presence that brooked no deviation from her plans. I can honestly say her organisational skills were exceptional and it is here I can give her at least some credit.

As with most unresolved clashes they can start small and then build to a climax. This particular Sunday morning I had the responsibility of hanging out the tea towels used for communion. On the way to prove myself capable of this task, a Christian brother beckoned me for his attention. I hadn't seen him for some time and one look at his face showed me all wasn't well.

" My wife committed suicide last month," he whispered as I was about to pass, planning to catch up with him later. Well, he had my immediate attention!

About a half an hour later a very unhappy Deaconess came stomping by and was wondering why the tea towels were not on the line. In fact she had to do them instead! I tried to explain that I still intended to complete my duty but a person's pressing need had taken priority. Sadly, it didn't seem to change anything so far as my duty. Her opinion of me and my reputation it seemed was always going to zero.

There were more clashes to come. It seemed we were pitted against each other when it could have been a complimentary partnership in the Lord. When I finally did leave the church (not directly related to this Deaconess) I felt convicted about my own responses. I sincerely wanted to do something to repair this breach but simply didn't know how. We had both moved on in different directions.

God is gracious and like the Hound from Heaven stayed on our case.

This particular day I decided to go into town. The O Bahn Bus near where we lived was a short trip of about 15mins. There was only one seat available on this particular day. Perhaps you have already guessed the occupant of this seating. Both of us were surprised as neither of us apparently took the O bahn regularly into town. The polite rather cordial conversation mostly revolved around what we doing now etc…

This lady's stop came before mine but I realized this was a God ordained opportunity. It was not to be missed! After alighting the bus together, I took a deep breath with a silent prayer for the brief conversation to follow. I cannot remember the exact words but it went along these lines.

I know we've had our clashes and disagreed on many things in the past but I'd like to wish you well in your present and future ventures. There was no great emotional outpourings or confessions. I did at least manage to hold her hand warmly and sincerely. She remained her stoic self but I felt this attempt to mend the breach was an important step in moving us both forward. We were never going to be close friends or even perhaps see each other again. I did hope we could at least close on a positive note and perhaps even pray for one another.

I hoped that I managed to convey my respect (a form of love). This too would allow God to continue His work in us both.

Conflict within any family situation is inevitable. In fact it is a normal and important part of our Christian growth. Our precious Saviour has already outlined in His Word and the example of His life, as to how we should deal with these conflicts. It may be hard to embrace conflict as an opportunity to grow into His likeness but when we do, the peaceful fruit of righteousness is our reward.

"Now no discipline seems joyful for the present, but painful; nevertheless afterwards it yields the peaceable fruit of righteousness to those who have been trained by it." (Hebrews 12:11)

There is no doubt that at some point in our Christian walk there will be more than a few sand paper relationships. Perhaps at least one without closure. I have found the following prayer helpful when I have done all that is possible in an effort to bring reconciliation but without reciprocation.

Lord Jesus,

I've done all you require of me. You alone hold the full understanding of this situation. Reveal any hidden faults on my part and let no root of bitterness take hold in my spirit. Help me to move on in your grace and forgiveness and allow you to work out your perfect plan for both of us. AMEN.

Not all breaches are mended promptly or in the way we would desire. Only God sees the bigger picture. None of us are finished articles and only God sees the intended pattern. We only see the underside of the crisscrossing tapestry. He asks only that we trust Him fully in each situation.

I have certainly appreciated the important and challenging role of Pastors and church leaders facing similar and often more challenging situations. What amazing patience, grace and sacrifice our Pastors and leaders exhibit daily which most of us take for granted. Some are called to manage mega churches in the thousands!

Our Pastors and Leaders need our prayers, appreciation and encouragement!

Walking in LOVE requires transparency. His agape love keeps us humble and pliable; allowing the Holy Spirit to grow us into His likeness. I firmly believe it is paramount in importance in every church or fellowship group. God wants His people to be REAL. He desires honesty. Not just in our day to day connections but honesty with our brothers and sisters in the Lord. Honesty before God and each other.

Another lesson I have learnt which is of equal importance.

It is possible to be right but handle that rightness in a very wrong way. God expects humility (disciplined strength) working together with unconditional agape love. This means remembering to press the PAUSE button despite the large green button looking a whole lot more inviting.

PRESS ON even if it's only a limp you can manage for now...

p.s. transparency does not mean we need to hang out all our hidden secrets to everyone all the time. God forbid! It does mean we need to walk in sincerity so that the Gospel is not hindered.

Chapter Six

WALKING IN ENCOURAGEMENT

"Encourage one another and build up one another, just as you are also doing." (1 Thessalonians 5:11)

Most persons on Facebook can boast of more than a few followers. Celebrities tend to have followings in the thousands and beyond. Donald Trump, the former U.S.A. President, boasts of a following of several million.

I wonder how many of these can be regarded as solid friendships. The kind that endure the test of time. Strong, reliable and slow to judge. Genuine friends are prepared to walk with us through both the good and bad times. Ready to supply a good report but also ready to confront us when we truly need it.

How many of these do you have? If you are like myself they probably add up to less than the fingers on one hand.

The finest quality I look for in friendships is ENCOURAGEMENT. We can never have too much encouragement. On the other side, too much praise can make us flabby and conceited. Encouragement builds up the spirit while praise may elevate the soul. When we keep this distinction, humility and grace become our most endearing hallmark.

Encouragement guards our soul from the enemy's arrows. It brings strength and steadfastness when self pity would destabilize and halt our progress in the Lord.

In the Book of Acts, the Apostle Barnabas is referred to as the son of encouragement. No other giftings are recorded of him. Although this doesn't mean there were none, encouraging the brethren was his obvious stand out asset.

We all need to have a Barnabas in our circle of friendships. If you can't find one, I exhort you to make it your aim to be one yourself. You will then never walk alone; God's grace and favour your cloak and staff.

I have only been attending this particular church for a few months. It is not a large fellowship but the people seem warm and friendly. One lady in particular seemed genuinely interested in myself (and indeed all newcomers to the church). In a very unofficial capacity she seemed to have made it her particular task to design handmade cards of encouragement and welcome. I love this encouraging touch.

Another equally genuine lady, makes it a point of getting to know the less popular people; those struggling emotionally. To make them feel special she buys them coffee and cake at a local coffee shop and endeavours to get to know them better on a personal level. This helps her know how to pray for them while building a bridge of meaningful connection.

Both these examples of seemingly small gestures of encouragement, I am confident have great effect in the Kingdom of God.

Another important point came to mind as I started to write this chapter.

There will be no doubt times in our lives when people and situations let us down. Tucked in between the graph of our highs and lows, there are hopefully more than a few plateaus of tranquility. However, no matter where we may be on the graph at any given season, it is good to know that we can always encourage ourselves in the Lord. Indeed, the lean times of drought allow the roots to go deeper in their search for water. Our faith muscles are strengthened.

Let us look to Christ Himself and draw upon His promises; discovering afresh that He is always faithful even when we are faithless. Even when those close to us, let us down.

How wonderful still.

The same God of the mountains is also God in the valleys. The God of the good times is also God in the bad times. The same God of the day is still God in the night.

He changes not.

PRESS ON: Keep walking in encouragement - especially as the Day of His return grows nearer.

Chapter Seven

WALKING AS ONE

"Now concerning spiritual gifts, brethren, I do not want you to be ignorant..." (1 Corinthians chapts. 12 & 13)

The Apostle Paul in his letters to the early church often stresses the importance of using the spiritual gift/s given to us through the Holy Spirit. These are not human talents granted and developed through our own particularly DNA or natural bent (Although I do believe God would desire they also be used for the benefit of the Body). The above are unmerited supernatural gifts meant to be used for His glory so the Body can move as ONE.

The picture of a body with loosely attached limbs all moving singularly without attachment or coordination is not an edifying picture. In fact it could be quite scary!

Claude Monet was a great painter with a unique style. According to some researchers his style came out of an increasing marked deterioration in the sight of one eye. One of his admirers made this very interesting observation.

"It was only one eye but oh what an eye!"

Our gift/s were not meant to be put on a display shelf or treated with false humility. Every gift is important and meant to be identified and used for His glory. Whether a pinky finger, the mouth or an eye, God wants us to use our gift/s and so advance His Kingdom.

However, two important points stand out.

Christ is the Head of the Body. The Central Tower whose directions need to be obeyed.

It is the Holy Spirit who both supplies and gives power so that the whole body may be edified.

It is the desire and joy I imagine of every Pastor/church Leader to see their flock in witness mode. Each one of us should be able to manage at least some sort of soft shoe shuffle into the fields ripe for harvest. Combined as One unit we are a formidable force to be reckoned with.

Many view church unity largely in terms of the melding of all denominational persuasions into one organization. The uniting together in the doctrinal things that are agreed upon rather than those doctrines that separate. In essence Truth will always divide and should never be sacrificed on the altar of any man-made unity. It is therefore imperative we know and rely on God's Word; keeping our focus on the author and perfecter of our faith- not the false ideals of man made organizations.

Both prophetic utterances and organized religion must always be tested against God's character and His Word.

True church unity comes from the Holy Spirit. It is the work of the Holy Spirit to provide supernatural gifts and power for witness so that we move as

ONE. The Kingdom of God comprises the true body of Christ; the expectant bride awaiting the return of the bridegroom.

There seems to be another disturbing trend in some church circles today. The most gifted or attractive are promoted and put on display; supposed evidence of the church keeping step with the world's bent. Look at our beautiful talented people! Join our super cool group! The 'seeker friendly' church does not reflect the true body of Christ. A very shallow picture of Christ and His body moving as one.

Indeed, Christ reversed the world's values. Read again the sermon on the Mount. The Gospel stories and the letters to the early church make it very clear the Kingdom of God looks very different from the Kingdom of the world.

"The world's estimation of "beauty" and God's evaluation of beauty in His people are sometimes poles apart. And we must recognize that often the rugged character and sterling soul shaped under the hand of God, beautiful to His eyes, may indeed be despised by His contemporaries." W.Phillip Keller.

Sometimes I listen to sermons on the ACCTV channel. This particular Pastor caught my interest while preaching on 'The reason for the need to meet in church.' (Perhaps numbers were down and a stern exhortation was now necessary). He did however, emphasize the need for the church to operate in the spirit of GRACE. He also listed a few other very important reasons including teaching and service.

However, at the conclusion of his message I felt something was missing but couldn't quite put my finger on the missing ingredient.

The next day while reflecting on the outpouring of God's Spirit in the Book of Acts the missing ingredient became powerfully apparent. I think the term is aptly described as a light bulb moment!

The disciples came together as a body with one accord. For one purpose. To praise and worship the living God who loved and gave Himself for them. Their praise and exaltation invited His presence. Invited Him to have total sway in their lives. They worshipped the one who was worthy of all praise and glory. His worthmanship was the centre of their worship.

Preaching, teaching and serving were the overflow of this worship, not the central focus.

Another equally challenging Scripture came to mind from the Old Testament.

The story of Job in the Book of Job records his response to a series of tragedies that follow each other in rapid succession. There is no doubt the weight of grief shook the very core of his being, including his own belief system.

However, despite his grief, his first reaction to the tragic news was the right response.

"Then Job arose, tore his robes, and shaved his head and fell to the ground and **worshipped.**

"Naked I came from my mothers womb, and naked shall I return there.

The Lord gave and the Lord has taken away:

blessed be the name of the Lord."

Job 1: 20

Having responded righteously (in the true spirit of worship) he was now positioned to hear and understand regarding the true nature of God and His purposes.

Despite the unhelpful counsel of well meaning friends, Job finally recognises the sovereignty of God. It surpasses Job's status and standing. It surpasses everything that relies on human effort to appease or please Him. The great *I am who I am*.

Job's huge cloud of flawed Theology continues to be drawn back like a cloak. Job humbles himself in the presence of God and is rewarded with spiritual sight.

True Worship involves the acknowledgement of God's worth-ship. Our finest service and ministries are only as relevent as our acknowledgement of Christ's power and victory over all His creation and circumstance. In both the good and challenging seasons He remains the same. His promises remain secure. Hallelujah what a saviour!!

To be anything less in our worship leans to lukewarmness. Lots of sincere Christians doing worthy service for the Lord but lacking Holy Spirit power.

None of us are meant to be mere church life spectators. The hunger for God's power not our own is a powerful catalyst for change. A hunger for God Himself. Only then can true unity through Holy Spirit power be released.

PRESS ON: Let us unite as ONE ; giving Him all the honour, glory and power due to His name.

Chapter Eight

WATCH AND PRAY

"Praying with all prayer and supplication in the Spirit, being watchful to this end with all perseverance and supplication for all the saints." (Ephesians 6:18)

If there is such a thing as a reluctant chapter. For myself this is the one. Reluctant not because I feel it is least important but because I feel least qualified to write it.

Before I started this journey I asked God to take me personally through all the areas that needed to be covered in this book. I did not want the book to be mere head knowledge or principles without power.

I thank God for all the conflict, trials and disappointments He has allowed into my life. I rather felt I had enough material to do a whole book on the last chapter. However I am not certain if a whole book on the topic of embracing conflict would resonate with every reader.

I do however, believe the Lord wants me to highlight the importance of PRAYER.

It is only recently that I acknowledged my need not to just pray but to pray with power. Pray believing before even receiving the answer. I even started reading a book titled: INTERCESSION, THRILLING AND FULFILLING by Joy Davidson.

I only got about a third way through the book and laid it aside. I didn't feel like an Intercessors bootlace, falling into the trap I had previously cautioned others about. Comparing ourselves and our gifts with others. It will do two things. Inflate us higher than we ought or deflate us to the point of discouragement. Don't go there!

What I do know is that Prayer is about His power and not our own; the culmination of our spirit combined with the purposes of God. God certainly still heals, delivers and even raises people from the dead today. Nothing has changed. However, I am convinced this may not always be His express will in every situation.

"The effective, fervent prayer of a righteous man avails much..."
(James 2: 16-18)

There are at least four things regarding the life of the Prophet Elijah worthy of mention.

Elijah possessed bold faith.

He cared about the honour and purpose of God.

He was in tune with the purposes of God.

He was persistent and expectant when waiting for God's answers.

When Elijah asked God to end the seven year drought in Israel, he sent out his servant seven times to check out God's answer. The servant reported on the seventh time that a small cloud the size of a man's fist was rising from the sea. The answer had come!

The account is in **1Kings 18: 41-46.**

Oh how I long to be that sort of prayer warrior. FAITHFUL... PERSISTENT...EXPECTANT!

I might add a footnote to the above. Elijah was not perfect. Like all of us he had flaws. His own fears threatened to render him ineffective but God chose him to do a certain job that nobody else would or could do.

Who can forget the dousing of water on wood that kept burning as Elijah challenged the power of the pagan god Baal? Yahweh, the God of Israel won the competition with no rivals. Then one squeak of retribution from the evil Jezebel, found Elijah running flat to the boards into the desert for fear of his life. He was so depleted in physical and spiritual energy He asks God to take his own life!

God did not give up on Elijah but after supernaturally providing practical refreshment (food and rest) he was ready at the right time to hear the still quiet voice of God in the cave. Elijah was gently brought to the place of understanding the true essence of God's power.

1Kings chapts. 18-19

Elijah's role was to seek God's face (find His will) and cooperate with God in bringing God's purposes to pass. I am glad we have his example.

God always answers prayer. He answers YES NO or NOT NOW.

There is no such thing as UNANSWERED prayer. The smallest utterance from the heart is not in vain. God cares for all His children and desires to offer them the best. He doesn't have favourites. Yes, sometimes the lines are temporarily blocked due to sin and unbelief. However, even here, the silence itself is often the answer.

The discipline of listening more carefully and waiting more patiently combined with expectant faith is easier to write than practice. I am however, already seeing some rather wonderful answers in prayer that can only come under the heading of MIRACULOUS.

Oh how I long to see more and more of His answers even as the Day of His return nears.

On the point of praying expectantly. My Husband Jack shared with me a significant experience re his time as Manager of a small stationery shop in Prospect, South Australia. Only a young Christian, he was faced with the daunting task of making monetary input match output.

On one occasion, a patron entered the shop with the need for a bill to be paid. Jack knew the person well enough to explain the money was not in the Bank at this point. (More than a few debts had to be paid to keep the shop flowing in its early days.) He told the person (a non-Christian) he intended writing the cheque out in faith believing the money would be available that same day. A bold move of faith indeed!

That same afternoon two persons came into the shop. One spent $1200.00 on stationery and other goods for his new business. Another came into the shop to settle a smaller debt. These two amounts came to just above the amount of the cheque he had filled out in faith!

EXPECTANT FAITH!!

Another part of prayer which I felt led to place in the Chapter heading of prayer is WATCH.

Seven years ago while dealing with a deepening depression, I felt the need to get another dog. Our Border Collie Cross had died several years before. Ben was a calm and mild mannered dog who never demanded much except food, shelter, a few pats and a daily walk.

The two dogs couldn't be more different. Corrie even as a small pup was a fiery bundle of affectionate hyper-activity. Part Kelpie and basset Hound is a dizzy combination. I felt stretched to the limit on just about every level. Her level of high sensory caused many issues which soon isolated both of us from the pack. She was definitely a field dog which meant long walks alone in challenging terrain. Anything loud or people and animals that seemed in the wrong place or unidentifiable meant I had to exert extra energy and alertness at all times to keep control. My stress levels went up instead of down. I resented being cut off from all the situations and fellowship with others I had hoped dear Corrie could bring to the table.

Now I view the picture somewhat differently. Corrie will always have challenging character traits but she is also protective and alert to my moods. I appreciate her attempts to give support during these times. I know she is highly intelligent and needs a firm hand and lots of activity for stimulation. I try to meet all these needs while recognising my own limitations. A huge balancing act!

The major discipline God has developed through my relationship with Corrie is the need to WATCH. I have to continually be on the alert and watch out for possible unpleasant encounters. Think ahead. Come prepared. Know the terrain. I am sure God has over-ruled more times than I can imagine. I also realize I need the discipline of sometimes being STILL and simply appreciating all that surrounds me and speaks of His glory and grace. This is covered further on in the book.

Today, more than ever, it is imperative to watch and wait expectantly for Christ's return. Matthew 24 is a chapter well worth reading. We do not know the hour or day of His return for good reason. However, we are exhorted to watch for the signs of the time that point to it. To be prepared and alert at all times.

To watch and wait expectantly requires a calm spirit.

Now back to Corrie who has mastered three commands which have provided albeit a small amount of control. SIT. STAY. CALM. Whenever her hyper reaction to things starts to get out of control, I now cover the three above commands with a simple CALM!!

I can't help wondering if this is also a command for myself. How easy to allow circumstance to rob us of our joy and peace. To indeed be watchful but then succumb to fear and anxiety; seeing only the waves instead of the One who controls the storm. CALM!

Before launching into prayer with all my needs, I now try to be first calm in His presence and listen for that still voice; barely audible above the clamour of life's demands.

God has a whole arsenal of things and yes, even people tailor made for our temperament and situation. Don't miss the thing that He is trying to reach in your life. Press the pause button and be prepared to see the things God wants you to see.

He knows us by name. He also knows the right tool to teach us things that will help us trust Him in both the big and smaller things of life.

Thank you Lord!

Before I conclude this chapter I feel the need to mention that there are all sorts of different forms of prayer. All have their place. Closet prayer, Prayer walking, spontaneous arrow prayers, Intercessory prayer, groaning prayer and also praying in other tongues.

Prayers of thanksgiving and praise deserve a category of their own in that they honour Him in a special way that invites His very presence into our hearts. This prayer form has very little to do with emotions. it comes from a will that chooses to see and honour Him in all things regardless of emotion. Sometimes fervent feelings follow, sometimes not. However, The determination to put Him first and acknowledge His power over our situation always brings favour and peace. The psalms of King David give clear testimony to this.

One of the finest records of a person praying is King David. It records that David sat before the Lord and prayed. I love this informal familiarity and expectancy. No technique or showy fluency needed. A faithful God and a sincere heart becoming as one.

PRESS ON in confidence. May our lives be a giant monument of steadfast prayer to a faithful God.

CHAPTER NINE

THE WHOLE ARMOUR OF GOD

"Finally my brethren be strong in the Lord and the power of His might. Put on the whole armour of God, that you may be able to stand against the wiles of the devil. For we do not wrestle against flesh and blood, but against principalities, against powers, against the rulers of darkness of this age...therefore take up the whole armour of God, that you may be able to withstand in the evil day, and having done all to stand.

Stand therefore having girded your waist with truth Put on the breasplate of righteousness having shod your feet with the the preparation of the Gospel of peace above all having taken the shield of faith quenching the fiery darts of the evil one. take the helmet of salvation with the sword of the spirit which is the Word of God."

(Ephesians 6: 10-20)

Most of the Apostle Paul's letters were either written from goal or house arrest. He would have been familiar with the Palace Guards and the kind of armor they wore. The Romans emphasized the need for physical might and power. The Apostle Paul reminds the Christian that the real battle is in the spiritual realm. The unseen principalities and forces whose main purpose is to disarm, discourage and deflect us from God's purpose.

The importance of properly securing our spiritual armor came home to me quite a few years ago during a church service. The message was on *'Putting on the whole armor of God.'*

To illustrate this Scriptural passage a cardboard cutout of a centurion soldier was erected and placed to the side of the pulpit. The soldier of course wore all the mentioned armory in Ephesians 6. A very gallant impressive construction used by the guest speaker who verbally re-enacted a scenario that fitted into the Biblical setting. This gifted man had obviously enacted this story many times over and his eloquence and sound effects held a captive audience.

Near the climax of his story, a strange thing happened. For no visibly conceivable reason the impressive helmet on the soldier slipped sideways over one of the soldier's eyes. There was a muffled ripple of laughter as the speaker continued, seemingly unaware of this stage prop mishap. He pressed on with fervent elocution. Only at the conclusion did someone restore the dignity of the noble soldier who at one point lost all semblance of nobility and we the audience had lost all sense of decore.

I now call it the 'unintentional message that stuck' unlike the soldier's helmet!

The soldier arrayed in all his battle fatigue would have been at quite a comic disadvantage if he'd turn to face the opposition with a slipped helmet. Even if he managed to secure all the rest of the important armor parts, this helmet slip would probably have cost him the battle and indeed his own life.

Prayer is more than just talking to God. It is also where the real battle begins and ends. A warfare that should involve every child of God. How foolish to go into battle without securing the helmet of SALVATION. Every armor piece has its place but the HELMET of SALVATION offers us the first and most important line of PROTECTION. Know who you are in Christ and believe you are saved and sealed by the Holy Spirit. Go boldly to the throne of grace and let your petitions be known to God.

We fight an opportunistic enemy whose strategy is to largely condemn, frustrate, tempt, and divide to keep us focused on anything but Christ Jesus Himself.

Another strategy I see being used very successfully in today's church on the war front, is the increasing tendency towards lukewarmness. The comfortable warmth of familiarity. The cosy nest of good people doing good things.

The passionate fire of the Holy Spirit is absent and one wonders even if it were powerfully ignited, would we cosey nesters recognize or even welcome this presence! The early church was never portrayed as a cosey nest for fledglings. Instead, this dynamic launching pad produced results so powerful, the world was turned upside down! However, in many parts of today's church it seems we have mistaken:

activity for spirituality

license for grace

purpose for spirit filled

mega for favor

religion for salvation

The great Evangelist Billy Graham is credited with saying,

"Ninety five percent of today's church activities would continue if the Holy Spirit were removed from us. In the early church ninety five percent of all her activities would have stopped if the Holy Spirit were removed."

A very sobering observation that very few of us could argue against successfully.

For some years now, I have been a supporter of the **OPEN DOORS MINISTRY**. Set up in the 1950s to reach the persecuted church with Bibles; largely smuggled into the underground church. It has now extended that mission to working alongside the local churches, assisting them with practical supplies and other forms of necessary support including prayer.

These persecuted Christians all over the world continually face death, destruction, starvation and a myriad of other forms of persecution but their faith is strong and their testimonies powerful. They rely on Christ alone and know that He is faithful. This is their testimony. This is their victory. Having nothing they have everything!

Some battles like the above are both spiritual and physical, often resulting in martyrdom. However, the fiercest battles largely arise from our mind and emotions. The unguarded corridors of power that unwittingly allow the enemy to roam free - The war relentlessly being waged within the soul in order to weaken the spirit.

Although the battle has already been won at the cross, the enemy roams around like a toothless tiger seeking to neutralize our witness and effectiveness. We need the whole armor of God to withstand an invisible enemy. Indeed, a persistent enemy who knows all the chinks in our armory and seeks to gain an advantage.

Having done all, the Apostle Paul exhorts us to STAND. Stand on His promises in His Word. Refuse to give ground to the enemy's lies. Raise our hands in praise to our victorious King of Kings and Lord of Lords. We actually reign with Christ in the Heavenlies. His royal blood is our defense. Let us therefore give no ground to the enemy.

"Therefore submit to God. Resist the devil and he will flee from you..." (James 4:7-8)

PRESS ON. Washed in the blood of the Lamb and fastened by the armor of Christ.

Chapter Ten

WALKING IN FREEDOM

There was a long break between the WATCH AND PRAY chapter. Once again the need to let the subject percolate. The book of Galatians was definitely worth another read and meditation. I encourage the reader to do the same because the contrast between walking in the flesh and walking in the spirit is the basis for this chapter.

"Having begun in the spirit are you now made perfect by the flesh..." *(Galatians 2: 1-4)*

The result of walking in the Spirit leads to true FREEDOM. The yoke of religious performance is lifted from our shoulders as we become new creations in Christ. Our obedience rooted and grounded in grace.

This freedom prepares us to be all that we are meant to be in Christ whose purposes can be fulfilled in our lives.

obedience without always seeing

Worship without always feeling

Giving till it hurts

Forgiving when it hurts even more

Praising Him in all situations

"Now back to the recent converts based in Galatia. Unlike those reliant on the old Judaic system of beliefs, the Christian convert is exhorted to move into a deeper walk with Christ Himself. I imagine this would not have been easy for those Jews converted to Christ in the Apostle Paul's time when the letters of the early Church were written. The Judaic system encompassed their whole life at every level.

How wonderful! Even here God had the situation covered. He planned the dramatic conversion of an orthodox Jewish Leader to show it could be done. Saul of Tarsus who became the Apostle Paul once thought it was honorable to persecute and put to death those who blasphemed and followed the man called Jesus. His personal encounter with Jesus Christ Himself dramatically changed that forever.

The Apostle Paul knew personally and powerfully what it meant to walk in the Spirit because he had spent most of his life walking in the flesh. A slave to a religious system that could not save him. A religious system designed to be the means to point to his need for Christ.

Yes, indeed he knew first-hand what it meant to make Christ Jesus Lord and Saviour and put to death what is earthly within. To be truly free!!

The flesh in this case involved more than just carnal desires common to us all. It involved dependence on the whole Jewish religious system to make clean the unclean. God required a circumcision of the heart not the flesh. The need to understand that grace supersedes the law. The law reveals our total inability to keep it. It is meant to point to the sinless perfection of Christ who sets us free from the law of sin and death.

Only the Spirit of God can produce such a change.

Thankfully, those of us not of Judaic origins do not have to grapple with such a radical change.

However, the root of religiosity which is spiritual pride is a challenge to both Jew and Gentile alike. To walk in GRACE : receiving His undeserved favour is often more difficult to embrace than works based religion.

This does not mean there is no place for rituals or visuals to remind us of God's grace. God is a God of order. He encourages us to participate in the ordinance of taking communion to remind us the true essence of the Gospel. Baptism by immersion to illustrate our new life in Christ. He exhorts us to use all His spiritual gifts for witness and God's glory.

It is our own religious tendencies that sometimes cause us to go further. Just like the Pharisees of old, rituals (or expectations) can be used to control rather than setting us free through grace. The rituals may not be wrong in themselves but they can quickly turn into idols when used for the wrong reason. The Holy Spirit is then grieved.

"...*Do not quench the Spirit. Do not despise prophecies. Test all things; hold fast what is good. Abstain from every form of evil."*
(1Thessalonians 5:16-21)

Every summer I do battle with a cheap hose whose water supply is often cut off when it is bent. This sharp kink (much to my frustration) immediately blocks any flow of water. In like manner on a spiritual plain, it is very easy to quench the Holy Spirit.

Only a few days ago I prayed for an opportunity to witness. When it did come I promptly quenched the Spirit and then tried to use a litany of excuses to cover myself. When the Holy Spirit gives a check in our Spirit we need to listen.

I have been in churches where Holy Spirit life has started to flow only to find the flow abruptly halted. Most often by well-meaning church leaders supposedly keen to protect their flock. The need to quickly halt anything that appears out of our control is not uncommon.

Sadly, some Church Leaders would prefer to throw the baby out with the bath water than to TEST everything. They fail to understand what it means to walk in the freedom that comes from GRACE and instead, resort back to legalism.

How easy to lose the freedom we have in Christ at conversion and go back to walking in the flesh. This freedom is not the same as the world's freedom. We must never forget we are bond servants to Christ - saved by grace-living for His glory. Grace is not an excuse to do as we please. When understood and wholeheartedly embraced, it lifts and propels us towards the upward call of Christ to be like Him and live in and for Him.

This in fact is true joy and true freedom!

We are not made perfect (complete) through our behavior. We are made perfect through our position in Christ! God's grace alone granted through His Son's completed work on the cross. When we allow the Holy Spirit to establish this truth firmly in our hearts it is hard to turn back to finding hope and freedom in the flesh.

It took some years of undergoing gentle but extensive chisselling, chipping and molding to show me just how pervasive the spirit of LEGALISM had crept into my own life. When I did discover this tendency and started to walk in FREEDOM it was not understood by everyone and even viewed as a threat by some.

The yeast of Pharisaism can indeed be so pervasive it can blind us to true spiritual realities.

There is something inherent in all of us that causes us to gravitate to that which we can touch and feel. The concept of WALKING IN THE SPIRIT could after all prove to be highly risky- wobbly emotionalism -putting feelings above rationalism.

On the other hand when we are sincerely walking in the freedom of the spirit, the above negatives are actually contained in their rightful place. Producing good fruit is the result.

"I am the vine, you are the branches. He who abides in me and I in Him bears much fruit; for without me you can do nothing."
(John 15:5)

Recently I noticed another tendency that God has personally seen fit to draw to my attention. The tendency to be a little casual and somewhat impatient when stressing Spiritual truths. This has led I am sure to misunderstanding by some.

I once told a dear Christian lady that I disliked the tendency to 'niceness' and 'politeness' by many in Christian circles. This lady looked somewhat startled and has avoided me ever since.

I did not qualify my statement. I am sure she imagined I meant I would rather church people be 'nasty' and 'uncaring!'

I actually meant the importance of Christians having a *genuine love* towards each other. The image of authenticity is very attractive to a world largely lured by the fake or superficial.

Oswald Chambers in his book 'My Utmost for His highest' phrased it a little differently. I am sure it still raises quite a few eyebrows.

'The enemy of God's **best** is often GOOD. Hmmn. Worth a thought.

God's best is for us is to be emptied of self and personal performance and filled with His Spirit. This is true FREEDOM.

To walk in the Spirit means being honest before God and each other. It is being real when it would be easier to hide. When we invite His presence into our lives, we receive His favour.

"If you really want to walk in His Spirit - if you really want His anointing - you need to ask more direction from Him...come into His presence...get to know His heart...His desires. He wants to anoint you to use you in His kingdom." David Wilkersen

PRESS ON. When the Son sets us free we are free indeed!

Chapter Eleven

WALKING IN SPIRIT AND TRUTH

The question. 'What is truth?' is an important one. It is here that all other questions re the Christian faith stand or fall.

"If you abide in my Word, you are my disciples indeed. And you shall know the truth and the truth shall make you free." (John 8:31)

Truth in essence is based on fact. All the major faiths at the very least acknowledge the existence of Jesus Christ. Most view Him as a great Teacher or Prophet. The well known Historian Josephus gives verification to the Gospel records of Jesus Christ death and resurrection. The story of Christ (and also the Old Testament) is by no means based on cleverly designed fables as many would choose to believe and circulate in secular institutions. Historians have already clearly verified the existence of Jesus and New Testament records.

There is also ample evidence in creation itself that points to a clear pattern in the Universe. Logic suggests that where there is a pattern there must be a pattern maker

One can accept these facts or reject them. God has also built that into His plan. Greater still. The truth He talks about in this context surpasses even Historical facts. It is based on His sovereignty. He does not need to prove Himself. He is the great I AM.

To believe and receive Jesus Christ as the Saviour of the world-the one and only way to the Father is largely where the sharp division occur. This truth can only be received by FAITH.

"But as many as received Him, to them He gave them the right to become children of God, to those who believe in His name. Who were born not of blood, nor of the will of the flesh, nor of the will of man but of God." (John 1:12)

We are so very blessed to have the inspired Word of God; the myriad of Christian helps which can also aid our Christian walk. However, let us never forget the greatest search engine in the whole universe. The Holy Spirit.

"Eye has not seen nor the ear heard, nor have entered into the heart of man, the things which God has prepared for those who love Him. But God has revealed them to us through the Holy Spirit. For the Spirit searches all things, yes, the deep things of God." (1Corinthians 2: 9-10)

It is certainly true that as humans the natural tendency is to only see what we want to see. It is an inconvenient truth in itself. Both a blessing and a curse. Many demand to see before they believe but God's Kingdom inverts this truth. *We see when we choose to believe.*

Faith gives us sight. This is the separating point from all others religions. The requirement to adhere to principles and be bound to their system demands acceptance based on human effort. This is not Good News!

Jesus Christ made important statement when He spoke to the Samaritan woman at the well.

He spoke of Himself as the source of never ending life and power. Not just at conversion but as an ongoing source that can never run dry.

"God is Spirit, and those that worship Him must worship in Spirit and in Truth." (John 4:24)

Sadly, many christians refer reverently to the Bible as God's Word of Truth but ignore the same content that references the need for Holy Spirit power!

During the time of writing this Chapter I decided to enlist some penetrating thoughts from sound Christian Leaders. After about a 40 minute browse on the internet, I felt totally sapped of energy and none the wiser.

Shutting down the computer, the scrappy mass of cuttings and some plants I had rescued from the local nursery on the brink of a near death experince, seemed suddely inviting. In fact it was they who rescued me from the onslaught of passionate Bible Teachers with equally passionate and often divergent Theological views.

Sadly, the dying plants taught me more than the commentary.

One struggling punnet of root bound lobelia almost died not from restricted space but drowning in the water I had placed them in-then promptly forgotten about. I gently placed them in a pot with another struggling lavender plant whom I discovered later was meant to be in a sunny spot rather than the shady spot I had chosen for them. Despite all my best motive only a song and a prayer could save them now.

The various plants and cuttings had at least found a home better than the damp plastic bags that had contained them for more than a few days. During this time I began to reflect on the lessons being shown by God.

Lesson 1. Good intentions do not get us to Heaven. We are saved by grace and grace alone.

Lesson2. Good fruit comes from abiding in Him. He only asks us to receive His grace and walk in His Spirit.

Lesson3. He is interested in our growth arising from our salvation. He knows the right soil plus the right amount of water and sun. We bloom best where He plants us. The right place for e all His provisions. Even when we are limp and at deaths dark door like my lobellia, the Good Gardener knows best how to bring growth and joy.

God is the Good Gardener (of our souls) as well as the Good Shepherd!

When we abide in Him and His words abide in us we can walk in quiet confidence. He wants us to trust Him with everything. The things we don't understand He promises to give clarity and guidance through His Holy Spirit.

The Scriptures provide the full revelation of God and indeed keep us grounded. Deception and counterfeit abound today. Some have departed, added onto, or subtly tweaked the truth to such an extent that it has caused spiritual blindness.

When we depart from foundational Scriptural truths we do it at our own peril. It leads to two extremes.

This stoic rigidity of denying the supernatural leads into legalism. The Bible (namely King James only edition) for some it seems has replaced the need for anything supernatural. They walk in truth but not in spirit. Some can quote and translate the Bible front cover to back but sadly often the presence of power and the warmth of genuine love overshadows their good intentions. Saved perhaps but lacking power.

"There are Christians who know all about God in a clinical way. They can dispute doctrines and discuss all the details related to Divine life. There is no end to the light they have, but it has never produced growth because it was not combined with a warm, personal love for Christ." W. P. Keller

(And I might add. A love for all those who differ with their own personal brand of Theology)

As sincere Christians we are known by the fruit of the Holy Spirit. Our best hallmark will always be our love for each other.

On the other side are those who readily embrace the supernatural. They readily, rely on Prophetic utterances without testing. However, without solid grounding in the foundational truths of God's Word, the counterfeit and all manner of excesses can weaken and even destroy faith. When the flames of emotionalism fade away so too can faith based largely on experiences and lacking solid foundational truths. God's wonderful promises to memorise and use as an anchor to the soul through changing seasons and shifting sands.

Both Truth and Spirit compose the balancing bar that keeps us stable as we walk the tightrope of faith.

Our natural tendency as humans is to gravitate to the extreme which feels the most comfortable according to our temperament. This natural temperament plus life's experiences tend to blur the lines of God's truth.

You see, it is the **God of the Word** not the Word of God that should be our central focus. The Word of God points us to the true source of power.

*"**Jesus of Nazareth was anointed by God with the Holy Spirit and great power. He did wonderful things for others and divinely healed all who were under the tyranny of the devil, for God had anointed Him.**" (Acts 10:38)*

Strangely, it does not say we put aside the personal filling and guidance of the Holy Spirit when we have the Written Word. This would be bizarre! Scripture itself gives testimony to the importance of the Holy Spirit as the presence and continuation of the same works of the Son before He ascended to the Father. The very presence of God who gives us *power, leads, searches, comforts, teaches, disciplines and also restrains…*

*"But when **He,** the Spirit of truth, comes, **He** will guide you into all truth; for **He** will not speak on **His** own initiative, but whatever **He** hears **He** will speak; and **He** will disclose to you what is to come. **He** will glorify me, for **He** will take of mine and will disclose it to you. All things that the Father has is mine; therefore I said that **He** takes of mine, and will disclose it to you. "*

(John 16: 13-15)

I counted and highlighted ten **HE** references to the Holy Spirit alone in this short section of Scripture. Therefore, to replace the Holy Spirit with the Scriptures is surely idolatry. Again, the only sin that is unforgivable is blasphemy of the Holy Spirit and more than a few Christian brethren swing very close to this sin when they mock and discredit workings of the Holy Spirit they do not understand.

I say this with great sadness knowing many are sincere in their fundamentalist beliefs.

Although criticized by some for having moved quite frequently to different places of worship, I view it differently. God has enabled me to gain a balanced picture of *these two extremes*.

Indeed, I praise God for the Baptism of the Holy Spirit. I praise Him for the faithful Ones that point us to His Word and provide a strong foundation. I also give Him thanks for the unexpected times of disappointment and discouragement that help my roots go deeper still. The dry and barren seasons when His presence seems strangely hidden. The gentle peace from walking in quietness and trust. The hunger for something more than mere lukewarm Christianity. The reliance on His Word more than the words of others.

The best lesson from all these seasons? To put no confidence in the flesh and view each success or failure as a chance to grow into Christ likeness.

Thankfully, both the Old and New Testament are actually testimony to people whose weaknesses were turned into strengths. This should give us all courage as we face a world (and some churches) who have equally distorted the image of God.

God will never allow Himself to be contained in our neat Theological boxes. Only in full surrender and faithfulness to Him is it possible to **"walk in spirit and in truth."** He invites us to embrace the full counsel of God (not just the parts that make us feel comfortable). It is possible then to not only **know** truth but to also **experience** truth according to the above verses.

Greater still is the knowledge that when we do see Him face to face, everything we now see dimly will then have perfect transparency. Perfect understanding. The place where faith finally becomes sight.

"For we know in part and we prophesy in part. But when that which is perfect has come, then that which is in part will be done away...For now we see in a mirror dimly, but then face to face. Now I know in part, but then I will know just as I am known..."
(2Corinthians 13: 9-13)

PRESS ON: Lord, fill and guide us with your Holy Spirit according to your Word.

Chapter Twelve

WALKING IN WISDOM

"And Jesus answered, and said to them. Take heed that no man deceive you." (Matthew 24: 4)

This chapter is not about exposing false teachers but it is about being aware of false teachings. It is not about personal opinion or pet theologies and philosophies. It is about knowing His Word as against the words of others. These may be good and accurate or false and misleading.

The Holy Spirit will guide us into ALL truth when we ask Him to help us discern truth from error. This calls for WISDOM. The wisdom that comes from above.

Today, even foundational truths are being questioned, twisted and tweaked. Theological cut and pastes by popular Preachers, Teachers and Theologians continue to infiltrate Christian circles. Many of these Bible Teachers appear to hold sound teaching and some may be sincere in their new found theories. However, when carefully examined, we see the major tenets of faith being questioned and rearranged, to form a palatable but erroneous narrative.

It is only too easy to mold Christ or the Gospel into our own preferred narrative. To sneak in a tiny intellectual appetiser that may fan the expounder's ego but weaken the soul. If we are to truly hold every thought captive, we must KNOW the Word of God and stick to it. Both content and context are important. Literal unless otherwise stated. Agreement in the hard bits regardless of customary norms.

Be wary of those who boast of presenting something NEW. This does not mean God will sometimes give us a new way of looking at an old truth. This is a healthy sign of maturity.

However, let's be clear. Neither eloquence or intellectual skill have high regard in the Kingdom of God. Examine carefully the teachings and measure them with the whole counsel of God's Word which does not lie.

The only way to recognise counterfeit is to be trained and well versed in the **authentic.** When in doubt go back to Scripture and steep yourself in truth. Not someone else's *version* of truth.

For many years Roman Catholic believers in the pre reformation era were not allowed to read the Scriptures for themselves. They relied on church leaders to guide and teach them. The words of their religious leaders were regarded as the final authority and were not to be questioned. This quickly led to excesses and a system that bound rather than set people free.

Thankfully, one brave reformer named Martin Luther stood against this system when he decided to study the Scriptures Himself. The Gospel truth of God's grace being freely granted to all those who received it through faith became a brave and radical encounter that shook the whole of Christendom. Martin Luther like all of us was not perfect but he did understand the perfection of Christ. *Saved and justified by grace through faith alone.*

The diluting of key words and terminology in some Bible translations has also subtly undermined the person of Christ and the Gospel. This is not to say that watered down Bible versions cannot be used as attention grabbers to those genuinely searching for truth. We should never underestimate His power to reach people in extraordinary ways. However, it is my firm belief that teaching and discipling, especially for new Christians should come from translations with the least amount of watering down or paraphrasing.

The New Testament letters constantly exhort us to be on our guard re heretical teaching. Perhaps we all need to go back to the pure word of God and both examine and heed these exhortations. The time of His appearing should not take us by surprise. We need to be ***ready***!

It is helpful to understand the relevance of Jesus's illustration re the Bride and Bride groom when we understand the Jewish custom regarding marriage arrangements.

The Bride and Bridegroom first sealed their arrangement before seperating for a short time.

The Bride would prepare the necessary clothing and household necessities while the Bridegroom would prepare housing arrangements. Neither the Bridegroom or Bride knew the day of the actual marriage ceremony but they both needed to be prepared. Thus the need for lamps to be trimmed and ready at all times.

The Bridegroom eagerly awaited the announcement day which had to come from the Father. When the day was declared, the Bridegroom would blow the shofar to loudly proclaim the imminent marriage with his betrothed. The Bride and her Bridesmaids would leap with joy and meet with the Bride Groom ready for the prepared Marriage ceremony and celebrations that followed.

The need to be ready according to **Matthew chapts. 24-26** must be taken seriously. There are varying views regarding end times theology but only the Father knows the exact time of Christ's appearance. Therefore the exhortation "to be ready" is important.

I believe the following statement re Christ's Return captures a sensible balance.

Plan as though Christ is never going to return. Be prepared and ready as if He is going to return today.

After a rather intense and somewhat revealing conversation with a particular Church Leader, I found myself reflecting on the state of the church today. Often much activity but spiritual vibrancy often replaced by mediocracy.

A busy church does not necessarily equal a spiritual church. Lots of activity can even replace the presence and power of the Holy Spirit. Like an endless spinning top it is easy to be diverted from the real thing. Busy reading interesting topical Christian books and videos. Busy doing benevolent works. Busy, busy, busy. In the midst of this busy spirit, truth is quietly being diluted or rearranged but we are often too busy to check this out when challenged. Content to do our spinning top performance; believing all must be well! Why? Because we're busy. Too busy to notice or rise to the challenge of the drifting tide of deception presenting a different Gospel.

Sadly, it sounds and looks very like the spirit of the Laodicean church in the Book of Revelation. According to Strongs Concordance, the Word Laodicea comes from two words.

Laos: meaning people

dicea: meaning rule

Another pitfall. The catchword for many fellowships it seems is 'tolerance.' Now I am all for tolerance of people. People from many different backgrounds, life experiences and spiritual maturity all make up the body of Christ. My small circle of close friendships, all coming from different Christian persuasions is testimony to this. However, I am not tolerant of false teaching. None of us should be. Thus my reason for inserting this chapter of warning.

The wolves continue to circle. Disturbingly, they look very much like the sheep but when confronted with foundational truths, their real characteristics are clearly not ovine.

The boat (nest?) might need a shakeup. Don't be afraid to give a hearty rock or challenge the direction it is moving. Do it **prayerfully** with wisdom and grace - also receiving correction lest we too fall into the temptation of missing out on God's best!

The Parable of the Wheat and the Tares in Matthew 13:24-30 is well worth another read. For some reason this parable kept rattling around inside my head after I thought I had concluded the chapter.

I had not read this parable for some time and a few verses I had originally glossed over as insignificant seemed to stand out. The following is a condensed commentary.

The Sower is GOD

The Harvest represents the WORLD

God's provisions are kind and generous, meeting all our needs. His children are His co workers within the field of mankind but note the following verse.

v.25 *"But while men **slept**, the enemy came and sowed tares among the wheat, and went his way."*

The task of sharing the spread of His Kingdom plan is massive. How easy to drop our guard while the enemy takes advantage as we sleep; quietly sowing poisonous seeds of division and heresy.

The tares and wheat continue to grow together and when they finally reach a certain height, the presence of the tares (which still may look similar to the wheat) start to emerge.

Greatly concerned, the servants mention this to the Householder, who seems undisturbed. He recognises immediatly the source of this toxic presence within His field,

v.28 *He calmly says to them. "An enemy has done this."*

Their own immediate reaction to deal with the tares was somewhat different. The tares needed to be ripped out now and then burned. Job done!!

Thankfully wisdom prevailed. Concerned that the good crop of wheat be damaged in the process, they are told to allow both the tares and wheat to grow alongside each other. When the time is ripe for reaping the Judge Himself will make the right call. The tares can then be seperated and put into bundles for burning. The wheat seperated and put into barns.

God is the only one who can judge with righteous judgement. This will happen at the end of this age. God's co-workers in His kingdom are called to discern false teaching and bring discipline to those causing divisions. However, taking the role of amateur judge is not our perogative. Only God can clearly discern the heart and motives of every human heart.

It is wise and prudent therefore to stay awake and be aware of the enemy's strategy to counterfeit. However, only God is fully qualified to administer the final judgements due to mankind.

The Year 2020 and beyond continues to cause great upheaval as the wheat and tares grow together. End time Prophecies are being fulfilled before our eyes. Freedom of Speech including Religious freedoms are constantly being challenged. Catch phrases like *'The Great Reset,' 'building back better,' 'We are all in this together'* all make reference to a better and safer world. This is the great LIE. WE (combined humanity) can make the world perfect.

The real truth is in plain sight-for those who want to see.

Apart from Christ we can do NOTHING!

It seems we are all being herded into the global pen, marked *'One size fits all.'* The concept of choice or any form of individuality is being steadily extinguished. The lack of respect for another's views both in the secular world and in some Christian circles is truly separating the sheep from the goats. The wheat from the tares.

Many seem blissfully unaware of the things to come. Some are willfully blind while others including those presenting as Christians, hold a cosy optiminism: quietly lulled to asleep as the enemy stealthily moves through the crop sowing tares.

I am reminded again by a saying I had not thought of for some time.

'Ignorance is bliss'

Ignorance may indeed be bliss-but only for a short time.

How then can we prepare ourselves as the gathering storm clouds continue to darken our path?

Once again I was reminded of Christ's example.

How did Jesus respond to the Devil's temptations when He was led into the wilderness?

He used the Word of God. Through the quoting of Scripture He was able to counter the subtle moves by satan to destroy His power base as Saviour of the world.

The enemy raided the line but failed to stop the goal destined to seal victory for all makind!

How much more does His church need to know and use the Word of God as a shield and protector of TRUTH? Having done all else to STAND. To stand on all the precious promises oulined in His Word through the power of the Holy Spirit.

How much more does the Bride of Christ need to be watching waiting for the trumpet sound that snatches her away prior the great tribulation. The time of the outpouring of God's wrath on a wicked, unbelieving world awaiting God's judgement.

Let us not faint (lose hope) but continue to pray, knowing we do not fight against flesh and blood but principalities and wickedness in high places.

Let us press on in love doing good in every opportunity that presents itself.

How do we fight?

We fight lies and deception with **truth!**

Let us indeed seek the WISDOM that comes from above. Indeed, when the world becomes darker, His people shine the brighter!

Godly wisdom also means being aware of the current Political climate. Global News outlets and social technology are all being primed to believe the narrative being presented. Half-truths. Fake news. Alarmist news. Disinformation. All these are being utilized to create and coerce the world to believe the great deception.

The popular narrative propagated by the majority should not be accepted without challenge. I believe it is important to get behind the mainstream news. Examine both sides and listen to the testimony of Godly people in High places.

We should certainly not make World News our MAIN focus. Nor should allow fear to shake our trust and disturb our peace. We do however, need to be aware of what is happening in the world and where we are being led. Jesus Himself exhorts us through the Gospels to look up and be mindful of the signs before His return for His bride. To look up and be ready!

The whole counsel of God through His Word is our most precious source of revelation. It points to Christ Jesus our Lord and Saviour who has provided His continual presence and power through the Holy Spirit. He is our shield and hope.

The nation of Israel is His timepiece to watch in these days to come. Scripture is being fulfilled before our eyes-for those who want to see!

The Book of Daniel

Matthew 24

2 Thessalonians chapts. 1 & 2

The **Book of Revelation** sets the stage for God's final judgement culminating with His return to earth with His bride. A New Heaven and New earth

PRESS ON: The truth is in plain sight-for those who truly want to see.

"Now to Him who is able to keep you

from stumbling,

And to present you faultless before

the presence of His glory

with exceeding joy,

To God our Saviour, who alone is wise,

Be glory and majesty,

Dominion and power,

Both now and forever."

AMEN

(Jude 24 & 25)

Chapter Thirteen

REJOICE ALWAYS

"Rejoice in the Lord always. Again I will say rejoice!" (Philippians 4:4)

The Greek word for REJOICE is *chara* meaning inner joy, delight or rejoicing. The Greek word for joy is similar. The word GRACE also comes from *chara* or *charis*.

Thankfully, this type of rejoicing does not always come from our emotional response to every given situation. Indeed our emotions may demand a totally different response.

Paul and Silas were held captive and chained to a wall in a filthy prison for witnessing Christ.

What was their response? They sung loud songs of praise. Wow!

What was the first thing Job did in the midst of his pain and suffering?

He fell on His face in worship. Wow!

Perhaps our own situation involves grief or loss. Anxiety and fear regarding the future. Depression in the present. Regret and confusion from the past.

Rejoicing in the Lord in the midst of a pain bubble is a disciplined mindset that comes from walking in the Spirit. Most often it comes not from our feelings but is instead activated by the will; a weapon against the the Evil One who seeks to capitalise on our pain. A powerful declaration of faith to God, ourselves and the enemy that we trust not in the circumstance but in the Ruler of the Universe. The King of Kings and Lord of lords.

Hallelujah what a saviour!!

Thankfully we are not asked to rejoice at every situation. This would be bizarre. We are however, exhorted to rejoice IN the situation.

To rejoice in the midst of each adversity releases the necessary faith surge to withstand the shaking of a disturbing reality. It offers God's PEACE and perspective.

The term. *'The dark night of the soul,'* aptly describes many of the valleys He calls us to pass through. This particular chapter challenged me at several levels. From commencement it spanned a good three months during which I faced my own valley of despond. I felt under attack from varying sources including health and circumstantial issues. The worst being my own inner negative chatter. My own name CAROL means *song of joy* but somewhere along the way I felt as though I had lost my song.

There were some encouraging patches that kept my head just above the water's surface but that's all!

I had always felt comfort in the Psalms of David who obviously experienced some fairly powerful highs and lows during his lifetime. However, no matter how low he descended, he always surfaced closing with a powerful acknowledgement of God's personhood and presence.

These meditations plus some beautiful uplifting songs of encouragement on YouTube became of great comfort. Strong reminders of God's faithfulness in my own trials

The need to reinforce my soul with encouragement and hope. The need to press on with confident hope not in people or situations but in the God of all hope who loves me with an everlasting love.

The comment. *"I've lost my Joy"* is certainly not uncommon. I suspect it is more common than realised though perhaps not verbalised. Sometimes I think our wise Heavenly Father allows us to go through lean patches where all positive feelings seem absent. I do believe these times to be very important for our growth. They help our roots go deep so that we mature and are able to withstand the lean seasons of drought.

I also discovered another important pattern.

Most of the passages relating to joy and rejoicing came out of a time of heavy trial. In fact Joy appears more an outcome than an emotion.

"...Looking unto Jesus, the author and finisher of our faith, who for the joy that was set before Him, endured the cross, despising the shame, and has sat down at the right hand of God." (Hebrews 12:2...)

Joyous song and dance both before and after each battle has been recorded as a hallmark of the nation of Israel. You could say it was part of their DNA. Their enemies knew this. When they were finally captured and defeated by the Babylonians they were recorded as hanging up their harps.

They had given up. The Babylonians had them on the ropes; mocking them by encouraging them to sing again their victory songs.

Psalm 137

As Christians we must not give into the temptation of losing our song (hanging up our harps!)in the face of trial and seeming defeat. It is at this very time, like the Apostle Paul and others, that we need to gird up our minds, and activate our song of praise.

A powerful declaration that the battle has already been won. Hallelujah what a saviour!

"And we know that all things work together for good to those that love God, to those who are the called according to His purposes...Who shall seperate us from the love of Christ? Shall tribulation, or distress or persecution, or famine or nakedness or peril or sword?...Yet in all these things we are more than conquorors through Him that loved us..." (Romans 8:28-39)

PRESS ON: Be thankful and filled with joy; wielding the powerful weapon of praise!

Chapter Fourteen

REST IN THE LORD

"**...My presence will go with you and I will give you rest.**" (Exodus 33:14)

Somewhere in the midst of this putting on the whole armor of God and wrestling with both seen and unseen forces, I was reminded afresh the importance of REST. Certainly, the weekly Sabbath rest and other general forms of rest granted to us in the normal flow of life are important. These should not have low priority because our Maker knows the need to give ourselves time to recharge batteries in order to function effectively.

However, there is another **rest** with an extra dimension which is even more important. The spiritual rest that comes from our complete trust in the Lord. A day by day, moment by moment discipline. The art of resting on God's promises and character- especially in the midst of activity, division, tensions and pain. That thing we call LIFE.

At this point of writing I was constrained to press the pause button. To let go of my own stress and discover afresh, what it means to actually ***rest in the Lord.***

The responsibility of being a Carer to two members of my family plus writing this book is a balancing act. Add to this Chronic Fatigue Syndrome flareups (arising from stress and chemical sensitivities) and you have a tailor made chapter. My own internal chatter from a fast paced mind also poses a challenge. I think there is even a name for this syndrome. ADD. Adult Attention Deficit Disorder.

Rest, as you can imagine is not a normal flow of my life. However, I do believe it is an important discipline in the life of every believer. God wants to grant us His rest in order for us to receive His power.

Thankfully I am not controlled by technological forms of chatter, preferring occasional face to face chats in a coffee shops or similar. However, for this younger generation in particular, these contact times via technological devices have become a necessity. sometimes with huge drawbacks. They can also be a tool of unwelcome, negative or frivolous communication. Left unchecked, they can tax, distract and even destroy: robbing us of the quality of life God intended.

I have since discovered there is even a term for Aussie teens, too scared to break up with mobile phones because of FOMO - the *fear of missing out*, new research has found.

My advice here is simple. Make sure you control the beast and not the other way around.

On the subject of internal chatter the Lord drew my attention to a picture of a baby asleep on his father's shoulders. For some reason it powerfully resonated with my topic of resting in the Lord.

Now babies have the knack of falling into deep sleeps despite noise and activity whirling around them. I enjoy watching Carols by Candle Light each year. Apart from the carol singing it has always been a fascination to watch small babies contentedly embracing the moment then miraculously-often at the loud climax of the Hallelujah chorus- nodding off into contented oblivium.

To fall asleep in the midst of such a loud culmination of noise and hype certainly has a lot to do with how God has physically designed them. However I can't help wondering if there is also a spiritual message here.

The *rest* spoken in the above Scripture has a lot to do with joy, contentment and yes PERFECT TRUST. A healthy baby or infant lacks the adult inner chatter of anxiety, insecurity, fear, guilt and aprehension plus a whole host of other negative input we adults collect along our life's journey. These are the things that can rob us of the rest God intends.

A healthy baby has three basic needs. Love (attention) food, and sleep. It sleeps deeply because these needs are being met. It is totally dependent on the Parent/s to provide this. It is an established fact within the medical professions that when these needs are not met a baby will soon grow into a fretful, anxious and disengaged child. The child then becomes an insecure adult with a host of other issues that often become powerful strongholds.

REST in the Lord can only come through perfect trust in a Father that promises to supply all our needs. We rest in His salvation and on His promises. Our expectations come from Him and Him alone. Like new born babes we must learn to REST on the Fathers shoulder and be at peace despite the tumult of troubles swirling around us.

Casting our cares upon the Lord is not a one off exhortation but rather a daily discipline that means focussing on Christ Himself. Like a small child or tiny infant we trust in Him to provide all that we need. Only then can we let all else fall as if it were nought.

I cannot say I have fully mastered this discipline even as I complete this chapter. I can say, that writing this chapter is an important step in reminding myself of that need. I can say, that when I let go of those situations (and sometimes people) that bring anxiety and unrest within, I experience a calm unexplainable peace.

"...Casting all your cares upon Him for He cares for you..."
(1 Peter 5:7)

PRESS ON. He knows all our needs and will never leave nor forsake us.

Chapter Fifteen

THE LORD IS MY SHEPHERD

I did not know how to end this book. I only knew it needed to be tied powerfully to what has gone before. **Psalm 23** came to mind and I knew instantly it was for my own encouragement and edification as well as the reader.

Now I can't help wondering how many hands would go up if the job of a shepherd/Shepherdess was on offer as a Career path. Perhaps some would find the job of herding sheep a satisfying challenge but I suspect it would never make it to the top ten popular career choices.

For those who have chosen a religious vocation I suspect the term shepherding sheep would perhaps qualify as a similar choice of career albeit with a lot more demanding layers of skill.

King David was the writer of this Psalm but historic details of date and location are fairly sketchy. I can confidently say that this was the right 'God prepared' career choice for David. I suspect as the younger brother, it probably wasn't even a choice. He did what was expected and made the most of every situation and learning skill that was available to him. Here are just some of those skills.

A Writer of verse and psalms

A Musical Instrument Player

A warrior of protection

An appreciator of art and beauty

A lover of the helpless

A nimble guide and sustainer

A Meditator and Muser of the things of God

All the above prepared him for the high calling of eventually being King of Israel. His first foray into this arena came with his defeating the enemy of Israel. Goliath the Philistine. A sling, a few small stones and a mighty faith in the power of the living God. Everything he had at his disposable he had learnt on the slopes of Judea as a shepherd boy!

Further, I am sure David the Shepherd boy knew the difference between a Good Shepherd and a hireling. Both did the same job but one did it with heart and vision. The other did it out of necessity for financial gain.

And yes, the sheep themselves recognized the difference. Studies have been shown to prove that sheep recognize the voice of the one leading them and are reluctant to follow a different voice. The Good Shepherd in return knows his sheep individually.

Psalm 23 is perhaps the most well know Psalm by both non-Christian and Christian alike.

Sadly, it is largely heard at funerals where it is often read in the context of death.

When I started to read Psalm 23 through fresh eyes I discovered something I hadn't really noticed before. It seems David intended it to be read and sung as a joyful, victorious prose to elevate our focus from the temporal to the eternal. God the Provider - Jehovah Jireh. The One who beckons us to follow Him on the journey of a lifetime - offering full protection.

During the time of preparing to write this Chapter, I experienced frequent nights of prolonged wakefulness. One particular night of wakefulness felt more like a full-on spiritual battle. The debilitating symptoms of being smothered and buffeted concerned me so much anxiety that on this particular night, I felt fearful of going back to sleep again. After listening to some beautiful song renditions of the Lord is My Shepherd my anxiety faded and the next night I was able to get back to somewhere near a reasonable nights sleep.

You see, I too needed to be reminded afresh.

The battle belongs to the Lord and because He is My Shepherd I can lie down in safety and know His protection.

It is my prayer that you the reader may also read Psalm 23 through fresh eyes. I suggest choosing a favourite version and reading it through slowly. Pause and meditate just like King David and let the words seep into your soul. I will comment on each line and may God lead us individually on the path He has already prepared for His name's sake.

He is the Good Shepherd.

'The Lord is my Shepherd.' Note the personal reference. Not A shepherd but MY Shepherd.

'I shall not want.' The sheep will have all their needs met.

'He makes me lie down in GREEN pastures.'

The Judean slopes are largely rocky with deep crevices and narrow trails. The shepherd has to know the terrain and then actively search out green tufts of grass- often tucked in behind rocks where the moisture from humidity helps growth. The western picture of sheep in knee deep green pastures does not accurately reflect the real picture of scattered tufts of grass on dry rocky terrain. The Shepherd scopes out this grass and provides only what is needed.

'He leads me beside STILL waters.' Sheep will only drink from still water…still waters are calming and bring restful contentment. What leads to our peace and satisfaction is often what we would not choose; that is why He is the shepherd and we are the sheep!

'He restores my soul.' The above provision brings quiet contentment and rest to the flock. In the same way our confidence in God's guidance and provision should also bring us REST and wholeness.

'He leads me in paths of righteousness for His names sake.' The Shepherd's reputation rests on His ability to provide, protect and give rest. This is why Jesus Christ is referred to as the Good Shepherd.

The shepherd often has to herd the sheep in cave-like rocky crevices to protect them through the night. Rocks are piled up to keep them in and the shepherd uses his body as a gate as he sleeps and protects them from predators. ***John 10: 1-18***

'Yea, though I walk through the valley of the shadow of death, I will fear no evil for You are with me. Your rod and your staff they comfort me.'

Particularly near the end of the day, shadows begin to cover the valley. This can be a scary and dangerous time for both the Shepherd and sheep. A time when the slopes and crevices become more treacherous and dangerous. A time of vulnerability as the light fades and moving shadows cast a pallor of fear. Death becomes more real but the gentle tap of the rod and loop of the staff give the sheep confidence that the Shepherd is there to guide and protect. Their passage is safe and fear is quelled.

'You prepare a table before me in the presence of my enemies; You anoint my head with oil. My cup runs over. Surely goodness and mercy shall follow me all the days of my life and I will dwell in the House of the Lord forever.

David seems to shift gears at this point. Showing confidence not just in God's physical protection but His spiritual covering of grace and unmerited favour. He is favoured in the presence of even his enemies and invited to feast on everything that is good. His cup spills over with generosity.

Every benefit that befits a King spills over to His children. Our GUIDANCE, PROVISION, PROTECTION and ANNOINTING is secured not just for this life but for all eternity. Our passage is safely fashioned and prepared by the Good Shepherd Himself.

"You will show me the path of life; In your presence is fullness of joy; at your right hand are pleasures forevermore." (Psalm 16:11)

Now that's really GOOD NEWS!

In the New Testament Jesus Christ refers to Himself as the **Good Shepherd**. This is explained in parable form Luke 15:1-7. His focus here is personal, illustrating His heart towards the one sheep that strays and needs to be found. The shepherd leaves the ninety nine to find the one that is lost. His greatest cause for joy and celebration is when the one that is lost is found!

Perhaps you do not identify with all the chapters that have gone before. You are perhaps not religious but you do recognise truth. The **Good shepherd** is **Christ Jesus**.

His invitation extends to all those willing to accept His offer of salvation.

"Come to me all you who labour and are heavy laden, and I will give you rest. Take my yoke upon you and learn from me: for I am gentle and lowly in heart, and you will find rest for your souls. For my yoke is easy and my burden is light." (Matthew 11:28-30)

PRESS ON in hope. He knows the way. Better still. He knows us by name. He will bring us safely to the place already prepared for us according to our faith.

He is the **Good Shepherd.**

Postscript

God speaks largely through His written Word but never in contradiction of it. In certain circumstances He also speaks in dreams and visions. Other times He directs us to what is happenning around us in the natural world. Testing circumstances are also meant to be important attention grabbers.

The still, small voice given to Elijah after all his mighty victories, taught him the most profound lesson of all.

God is in the simple and mundane as well as the large and dramatic.

I have already woven many illustrations throughout the chapters of this book. However, the following illustrations came after completion of the main body.

Every morning (and sometimes in the afternoon) a small magpie would do a few flying circuits around the garden, land on the ledge and peck a few times at my bedroom window. I know to the trained eye of the bird enthusiast there is some perfectly good reason for such a regular ritual. However, for some strange reason its presence always encouraged me lifting my often weary body and soul. A beautiful reminder of the presence of God in all our circumstance and seasons. That God is mindful of every sparrow (and magpie) that falls and will provide our every need.

Another time while walking in the foothills of South Australia, I observed an uprooted tree in a narrow area of the River Torrens. This huge gum tree had most of its root system jutting up out of the river. A bulwark of sand, stones, glass and all manner of debris accumulated from the riverbed. The uprooted tree slowed the flow of the river but apparently there was enough rootage in the river bed to allow a strong branch of the tree to still bring forth growth despite lying prostrate in the river.

Another smaller tree a few metres from the river source had less rootage and was not so fortunate in survival; succumbing to a dry summer.

God plants and expects growth. Our growth is dependent on the depth of our root system. If it is strong and deep it can sustain the occasional storm or drought. Even when toppled and seemingly defeated it puts out growth. Bowed but not defeated.

My final illustration comes with the basis of this book. It speaks of the importance of having a firm foundation. This **foundational faith** means being strong in the midst of an unstable world.

The following illustration is linked to the above

The note that came in our letterbox a few months back was not greeted with enthusiasm. The house over the road was being demolished with a risk of asbestos drift. Now waking up at 7am in the morning to trucks and heavy machinery did little to excite my already sagging energy levels.

I grumbled inwardly and could find no positives. My small industrious mapie seemed unfazed. Life for it continued as usual. However, the Lord did draw my attention to an important truth. A correct foundation is important.

Large machinery had to dig deep and remove all the foundational debris from the previous house. The amount of soil debis I'm sure would have been an archeoligists dream as birds excitedly converged on it regularly to cart away their treasures.

Everyone seemed happy except yours truly!

God is patient. He knew my pity party would come to an end. Only then could I see the truth He was trying to imprint upon my spirit. Namely, the importance of a solid foundation.

Jesus Himself uses a parable to illustrates this in **Matthew 7:24-27.** He references the building of two houses. One being built on a strong foundation withstanding the storm and the other house on a weak foundation folding quickly in the time of adversity.

This digging up of the old foundation ready for the new houses being in our street required massive soil and rubble removal. Before the cement for the new foundations could be poured, meticulous surveying and measuring was also required.

I can't find an exact verse to back up the following observation in relation to the above but I am confident it is accurate.

The process of being born again requires not only a new Spirit placed within to replace the old. It also means the need to allow God to dig up the old foundation. The hidden debris within that no one but Christ can see. It all all has to go. Thankfully not over night but at the pace and depth we allow God to work within our soul.

Thankfully, not all God's chosen instruments recorded in His Word were perfect but they do show us the importance of having an undivided heart before God. The importance of having a firm foundation that enables us to walk faithfully before God in every season of life till he finally calls us Home.

BE ENCOURAGED

FAITH grows amid storms. Right in the midst where it is fiercest. You may shrink back from a fierce storm of trial...but go in! God is in the centre of all your trials, and to whisper His secrets which will make you come forth with a shining face and an indomitable faith that all the demons of hell shall never afterwards cause to waver.

E.A. Kilbourne

EXTRA RESOURCE

YouTube: Unmasking the Great Reset: Jan Markel/Olive Tree Ministries

YouTube: The Signs of the Times: Our Daily Bread

YouTube: Pastor Jack Hibbs: The Great Put On

www.ingramcontent.com/pod-product-compliance
Lightning Source LLC
Chambersburg PA
CBHW041926090426
42743CB00020B/3452